Late Autumn at Dumbarton Oaks

Other Works
by Johann M. Moser

Verse

Most Ancient of All Splendors

Farewell … and if Forever
And Other Poems

Prose

The Ivory Fount
A Novel

Love of the Blossoming Hills
New England Stories and Sketches

Tutelary Presences
And Other Stories

The Song of the Eternal Aeons
A Phantasmagoria

Translations

O Holy Night
An Anthology of Classic Nativity Verse

Devoutly I Adore Thee
Prayers and Hymns of St. Thomas Aquinas
(with Robert Anderson)

Johann M. Moser

Late Autumn at Dumbarton Oaks

And Other Poems

The Diamond Ledge Press
Sandwich, New Hampshire

For more information, please contact us at:
https://diamondledgepress.com/

978-1-964001-09-8 (hardback)
978-1-964001-10-4 (paperback)
978-1-964001-11-1 (ebook)

Library of Congress Control Number: 2024904674

Contents

Late Autumn at Dumbarton Oaks

Washington, D.C.

Northern winds from the Potomac
 Assail the autumn groves of Dumbarton Oaks.
Gravel paths are damp with rain.
 Dark clouds, forlorn in tempestuous gales,
Sweep beyond the wrought-iron gates,
 The Georgetown wharves and hills of Arlington.
Solitary ensigns flutter
 Over the domes and monuments of the city —
Austere sentinels of the Republic.
 But I have trod the pathways of this garden.
Mossy arbors shelter me.
 And I watch the black Dumbarton squirrels
Burrowing in the leaf-strewn lawns.
 They do not mourn the perishing year.
They cherish what has been given them.
 And they shall abide.
For I recall again, and yet again,
 Among these antique yews and cedars,
Liberty's just covenants,
 Rooted in nature, truth, and reverence —
A polity of virtuous distinction;
 Wherein ivy-mantled cornices still evoke
Auspices of a perpetual peace:
 Sovereign nations bound in comity forever.
And I behold once more
 Those rustic wheat-sheaves, hewn in stone,

Enshrining a hallowed precept:
    "For as you sow, so shall you reap."
Sparse rain sprinkles
    Weathered urns and wilted flower beds.
Fountains are drained for winter.
    Bare rose vines, looped from faded trellises
Tremble in the cold winds.
    But I find solace in the alcoves of this garden.
Lofty oak trees summon me.
    And I watch the black Dumbarton squirrels
Gathering acorns in the thickets.
    They do not dread the impending night.
They entrust the good that has been their own.
    And they shall abide.

Études: For Shakespearian Voices

1.

Aubade

Welcome the winsome dawn in eastern skies
Who tints the clouds with rose-gilt damascene,
Enjoining larks to rouse the turfy downs,
The garden paths, and leafy greenwood trees
Bedecked with drowsy coronets of dew.
With fingers fine she weaves the silky webs
Of this bright morn. She does not tarry long.
While here with veiled and slender arms she stoops
To savor amber cordials in their cups,
The sun, bright-crested, proud in majesty,
Fastens the golden cincture of the earth
And shakes the starry mantle from the sea.

2.

Chansons des saisons

SPRING

Brash spring unfurls its pennons to the sun!
Arrayed in sterling casque and crystal targe
It summons the earth to bright emblazonings
With all its benisons so richly clad.
Orchards bloom o'er fields scarred by winter's blight;
Dark coverts in the woodlands yield their store.
Moist papillae bud to the warm susurrus
Of a noontide breeze; vernal asparagus
Prospers, rooted deep in fecund soil.
As spring abounds, it hastens to avow
The violets and rhubarb at the gate,
The nimble fawn upon the mottled hills,
And vine-looped pools, where pale cygnets glide
Like pensive clouds mirrored in blue skies.

LATE SUMMER

Spades, mattocks, leathern tackle, brindled corn
Betoken entrance to the grange's store.
The woodbine curls above in shady trellis;
Among holly leaves, ruddy berries glow.
An oaken door swings wide on massy hinges
Into vaulted depths of warmth and fragrance.
Brass-hooped kegs, wooden hutches, potter's ware
Clutter the grange's gnarled and rough-hewn floor.
From the rafters, sides of smoke-blackened ham
Throng in muted rows and congregations
Like sober aldermen, distinguished sires,
Attending guild-hall of a Sabbath eve.
Staves of fallow sunlight slanting downward
From tattered eaves and roof-joists through the dark
Fret heaped and globèd pumpkins in their bins.

A rimless wheel, its usage long forgotten,
Projects its beveled spokes through dusty hay—
From spoke to spoke a hoary spider mends
Seams and tokens of rustic heraldry
For all these coffered liveries condign:
Cogs, curds, curds and sod, orbed and glossy plums.

AUTUMN

Sere earth now droops her peerless ensigns down;
In crimson conflagrations she resigns
The solemn forests to the north-wind blasts.
Icy ringlets nightly fringe the woodland pools;
Alder stalks rustle sparely in the breeze.
Above the fields, the sallow, brooding sun
Imparts long-tapered shadows to the land
And warmth ephemeral, whose mellow haze
Blanches hazelnuts and ripens honeycombs.
Pale meridians of the year decline;
Spindly starlight frosts the autumn night.

WINTER

What steaming pottage, heavy with earth's savor,
Shall bereave ravenous winter of its bite
And, at the trestle, quell the long night's pall
With fulsome countenance and seasoned tale?
The hearth beneath the holm-oak warms our den
Under its downy coverlets of straw;
The winds befriend us, as they lull and sweep;
Overhead the crystal spheres, churning to the west,
Entreat a coy and russet dawn to tread
Across these frozen hills, while unperturbed
We sleep—but in the woodlands far away
A stag uplifts his spiked and snowy branches.
Shrugging amain, he hails the morning sun
In translucent cape and bejeweled crown.

3.

Petite chanson d'amour avec bourdon

My Phyllis fine, she is so fair,
She dances on the dappled air;
Her sprightly brows and silken hair
Frame with gold her sapphires rare.
    Burden: "Her eye is swift, her foot is fleet."
    For I would all her love entreat.

My Phyllis veils her shoulders bare
With fragrant flowers so debonair
That she is worshiped everywhere
But does not heed my rueful prayer.
    Burden: "Her eye is swift, her foot is fleet."
    She spins for me my winding-sheet.

4.

Sonnet

Be not sad, wastrel Love; and do not mourn
A tender interlude both rare and fine:
This moment shall outlive its brief sojourn
And constancy shall be forever thine.
Time's dark and surly pageantry may chide,
Its livid shadows flitting on the wall,
Where only fretful images abide
Whose waywardness bequeaths a deathly pall.
For if, poor Love, thy orphaned ways confound
The gaudy destitution of the world,
Then from thy tattered garments shall redound
All glory to the firmament unfurled—
That in one precious moment thou canst bind
What all the ages seek and cannot find.

5.

Soliloque tragique

How shall our grievous utterance presume
To blunt and spurn the guttered panoplies
Of this giddy and importunate age?
What drear tendentious rites shall timely bide
Ruin of prospects, once so meet and clear,
Whose keen angelic eyes had not yet grown
Bedimmed, benumbed, and disposition bent
To pluck sad figs amid death's peevish grove?
Let antic fortune minister its gall.
Let all dominions prattle in the dark;
Let them cuff and batter churlish reckonings
To marshal in array voracious hordes
That with their cloven guidons spur apace
The inauspicious host, grim chariots
Barbed and smoking in the maze of war.
Behold, the heavens pelt the earth with hail;
Winds assault the sullen continents.
Banners flutter over gabled rooftops
And bastions of this disconsolate world.
But, not improvident, we shall surmise
The harbor's estuary, the sought repose.
Thus fraught and bound with lading to the shore—
With hawsers taut and anchor deeply cast—
We shall replenish yet our eager hold
And durance make both luminous and bold.

6.
Fête champêtre

Let's sunder now the vintage cask
And pass the ale in sportive flask!
The sheaves are bound, the granges latched,
The grain is husked, the roof-beams thatched.
The flocks are gathered from the hills,
And foison every larder fills,
Pressing out the bounteous sap
Of ripened buds in youthful lap.
Summoned by horn to village fête
The lads and maidens congregate
To dance about the dapper lout,
To tweak his nose and make him pout
And hie across the pleachèd glade
To snatch the apples in the shade.
The jocund pipes and fiddles prate
As drums and tabors syncopate;
In floral garb, pert Janet skips
While Giles the joiner downward trips,
Knocking over the festive board
Of harvest sweetmeats lately stored.
Hear stout and wrinkled Katie scold,
Watching her gamesome feast unrolled!
Tom and Jenny cavort and scream
To see the hounds lap up the cream.
At eventide in cherry skies
Roisterers of the earth arise
To cluster in tumultuous throng
Of universe gone mad in song.
Among the clouds at merry pace
The skittish stars play steeplechase.
The moon bends over cheery-eyed
To gape across the countryside

Where upside down and all awry
Intunes the fabled angels' cry
Who in sweet melody sing of
The wonderment of joyful love.

7.

Voyage fantastique

Antique mariners sailed beyond this horn
Of brass and ivory mounted at the rim
Of tractless ocean streams. Their valiant keels
Scooped and furled the tilth of swelling floods,
Their hulls threshing dark, tempestuous climes
To bays becalmed and fiery tropic zones.
Here cliffs of azure coquillage were poised
Upon the marge of inhospitable tides
While speckled dragons, in the deep, surpassed
The surge and wrack of wayward promontories
And green-tressed maidens lured with golden eyes,
Whose lays enticed to cloudy parapets
Lithe barques that lolled on hushed and sapphire seas.

8.

Envoi

To thee alone, of whom I here indite,
I commend these modest verses; to thee,
Master of true Revels, who yet beguiles
That sovereign pith and balm of all our days,
I extend my tribute; to thee, none other—
Friend, fellow guildsman, "Sweet Swan of Avon."

Songs of the Ancestral Lands

1.

The Boatman from Kerch

In turquoise bays and pine-girt coves
And inlets of oleander groves
His wide-planked prow is often seen
Slicing the ocean's sunny gleam.
His mast is tall, his gunwales long,
His seaward eyes are brisk and strong.
With stalwart strokes he parts the tides.
With gulls and hawks his heart resides.
Cold rills from mountains glazed with snow
Feed palms on shorelines far below.
Gusts from gorges sunder waves;
The sun splits clouds with fiery staves.
> *O where has he gone,*
>> *This boatman from Kerch?*
> *O where has he gone from me?*
Beyond the gray beaches,
> Beyond the white waters,
Beyond the dim Gates of the Sea.

Past windy headlands he steers his skiff
Skirting the harsh and precipitous cliff;
Rudder and oar he handles with ease
Churning through currents and impetuous breeze.
He laughs at the spray of the billowing swell;
Over scrolling crests, his sinews excel.

Casks and lading are harnessed with rope
As he scuds on a swale's tumultuous slope.
Pomegranate sunsets emblazon the land.
Ivory sea-scurf tassels the sand.
Hot winds, like blades from the desert, pierce
Tempests from tundras, chill and fierce.
    O where has he gone,
        This boatman from Kerch?
    O where has he gone from me?
Beyond the gray beaches,
    Beyond the white waters,
Beyond the dim Gates of the Sea.

2.
The Volga

O Mother Volga,
    How can we heed your silent plea?
Birches perch like chalk stockades
    Atop your arched and virid banks.
Sheaves of gilded domes
    Hover over larch groves in the mist —
A pilgrims' port and refuge.
    Distant dust-spouts coil and twist
Across these wind-scarped plains
    Like wiry Scythian armbands from of old.
Did Noah cast his anchor here?
    Did Solomon's crimson chariots greet
Brazen dragons from the East?
    Shall altars languish desolate and rare?
An otter slithers downward
    Into a pollen-stippled pool;
Its muzzle cuts a wedge of ripples.
    A heron stalks among the reeds.
Sturgeons in the roiling flood
    Glide southward from remote taigas.
Heraldic monumental beasts
    Crouch beneath the threatening skies.
A merchant opens coffers.
    A drayman yawns, nods off in sleep.
Horses snort and stamp their feet.
    A tiny barge indents the pale horizon.
Behold, Tsar David on a griffon
    Strides abreast these fire-rimmed steppes.
His scepter sparks with lightning.
    He flays the sun with triple swords.
His throne is in the whirlwinds,
    Clouds are dust beneath his feet.

His snow-white falcon, high above,
    Is drenched anew in blood-red dew.
O Mother Volga,
    How can we hearken to your prayer?

3.
Carmarthen

Thou, most beautiful, Carmarthen!
    No acorns like to thine,
No salmon spawned in upland streams
    Like to thy salmon sleek
In thy sleek currents swift and cold!
    No oaks upon the hills
Raise leafy heads as tall and dense.
    Along the windy coast—
No heather like thy purple downs,
    Thy purple headlands high
In mournful gales and stormy seas!
    Beautiful thy berries,
As ravens' eyes are black and clear,
    So black thy berries grow.
Matchless thy ponies' heft and stride
    Where on the beach at dawn
Their hoofbeats tread the ebbing tide.
    Let none presume to praise
Their own deep glens and cloud-filled skies
    Whose beauty shall not boast
More loveliness, O Carmarthen,
    If then compared with thee.

4.
My Little Horse

We trek through dusty valleys
Where condors on their wings
Glide over cloudy highlands,
Where the lonely *lobo* sings
And bright-beaked eagles fly:
    My little horse,
My little horse and I.

Our guitar is the palmetto
Whose fronds the breezes ply.
Our ponchos are the pampas.
Our sombrero is the sky
Whose spiraled sequins never die:
    My little horse,
My little horse and I.

Our beds are grassy canyons;
Our pillows rocky heights
With cacti watching over us.
Our blankets are dewy nights
That dawn spreads out to dry:
    My little horse,
My little horse and I.

We pan in high sierras,
Sifting gold from sandy streams
As cloud banks blink in thunder
Where we wander in our dreams.
We don't pause to say goodbye:
    My little horse,
My little horse and I.

Someday upon a mountain,
I know our paths will sever.
You'll set your eyes on distant lands.
Adiós, my friend, forever.
We do not need to cry:
  My little horse,
My little horse and I.

5.

Alpine Nocturne

Snow-fields above disperse the light
Of moonlit sky and starry night
Whence lulling breezes gently sluice
Through the woodland's fir and spruce,
Stirring forest eaves' dark brows.
Towering peaks' uplifted prows
Engird the lucent stars around
In icy chaplets hedged and bound.
Mossy rocks and stunted pine
Trace the rambling timberline.
In ravines of wind-swept trees
Chamois doze on folded knees.
Edelweiss petals on a ledge
Nod beside the chasm's edge.
Distant gorges far below
Surge with glacial torrents' flow,
While, nearby, the night-owl's song
Echoes the midnight chapel's gong.
Mists from pastures, steep and plush,
Slip down into the valley's hush
Enshrouding all the hamlets deep
In brooding coverlets of sleep.

6.

Bordighera

After Monet

Let carillons and belfries' praise
Embolden heaven these fine days;
Pink-brindled mountains, buff and green;
Fronds below, high-plumed, serene,
Sun-swabbed, sun-scorched, yellow-blue,
With fiery tussocks' tinted hue.
Let steep hill towns be bleached and lean,
Lime and ochre, aubergine.
Let fluted turret, flange, and spire
Through damasked organdy aspire.
Let old alembics, chantries' chimes,
Above those tufted blooms betimes
Regale that garnet eye so nigh
Pealing in the morning sky.

Barn Sale

New Hampshire, late June

Cupboards, prints, posters,
               Old coins and medals;
Antique dolls, sap-buckets, pewter frames;
          Lanterns, sleds, powder-horns;
Books, door-stops, copper kettles,
          Cow-bells, snowshoes, cast-iron toys;
Ice-saws; fiddles;
               Stoneware crocks,
Cranberry, lemon, cherry glass,
          Buckles, buttons, leather tack;
Bibles, bridles, yokes and antlers,
          Butter-churns and spinning wheels,
Horseshoes, jugs, pitchforks, tools.

               TODAY ONLY:
               FRESH STRAWBERRIES!

Pup

What gratitude would I not give
To have you, Pup, back home to live,
To see you coursing o'er the field
Or through the brushwood half-concealed.

The hall and hearth are not the same
As when you dozed before the flame,
Heeding in dream the sounding horn
Or chasing woodcocks from the thorn.

Your hazel eyes and golden fur
Would autumn pastures yet bestir.
Your life was filled with vim and grace;
Your love could all my love outpace.

Beyond these hills I know you run,
Beyond the thickets of the sun,
Where ages hence we'll reunite
In boundless forests ever bright.

Kedi

In memoriam

What! Swat! ... Pepper! Sass!
   Leap, catch!
      Grip and scratch!
Scrape the window!
   Pry the sash!
      Clasp the high metallic latch!
Peerless huntress,
   Scoot and tatter!
Bouncing flurry,
   Pounce and scatter!
Draw!
   Paw!
      Claw my keyboard, flick your tail!
   Nab my tab and click my mail!
Snap the hatch!
      Bat the pennies on the mat!
Grapple, scrape,
      Unravel every twine and tape!
Plucky, dappled,
        Sassafras!
      Entrap the shadows on the grass!
Ensnare shoelaces in a scrap!
   Leap like a fury in my lap!
        Wake me from my noontide nap!
   Snatch and fetch away my hat!
Scrappy tabby,
   Matchless cat!

19

My Paper Flower

Wispy wings of columbines
Glide through woodland shades.
Ladies' slippers, daffodils
Sough amid the mallow blades.
    But, O Ages Past,
        O Ages Past,
    Who has bestowed on me of late
            My paper flower,
        My poor paper flower?

Morning glories climb the fence.
Violets are drowsy in the spring.
Chorales of roses on the hills
Their radiant anthems gladly sing.
    But, O Present Age,
        O Present Age,
    Where shall I repose once more
            My paper flower,
        My poor paper flower?

Hummingbirds and butterflies
Glimmer in the noontide air.
Golden blossoms of the clouds
Entwine the sunlight's flaxen hair.
    But, O Ages yet to Come,
        O Ages yet to Come,
    When shall I retrieve afresh
            My paper flower,
        My poor paper flower?

Warranty Deed

Elderberry Farm, New Hampshire

From pin in rock
at point of beginning:

Thence northwesterly about one hundred and eighty feet
to cherry tree growing out of a stone cairn;

Thence westerly about twenty-three feet
to sugaring house (roof blown off in winter storm, never replaced);

Thence northerly about forty-five feet
to duck pond surrounded by white birches;

Thence northeasterly about eighty-five feet
to foundation of barn (burned down, February 14, 1934:
tasty mushrooms available here in late September);

Thence northerly about fifty feet
along stone wall and overgrown apple orchard;

Thence easterly about seventy-eight feet
to rusted harrow at edge of hay field
(Dan Casey's harrow, not much good for anything anymore;
'course, Dan Casey's not much good for anything anymore neither);

Thence south-southeasterly about one hundred and sixty-four feet
along ravine bordered by pines and blackberry bushes;

Thence easterly about seventy-five feet
to abandoned well (uncapped — don't fall in!);

Thence south-southeasterly about twenty feet
to footbridge over Moriah Mountain brook;

Thence southwesterly about one hundred and ninety-two feet
along old cow lane (no more cows, clogged with briars and nettles):

To pin in rock
at point of beginning.

Moritat

Welcome the gang that grinds the grist.
They know just whose arms to twist.
They know just whose throats to cut.
Welcome the gang that digs the rut.

Welcome the gang that kills for hire.
They know how to stack a pyre.
They know how to lop a head.
Welcome the gang that reaps the dead.

Welcome the gang that can rail and hoot.
They know how to heist and loot.
They know how to drain a vat.
Welcome the gang that can preen a rat.

Welcome the gang we can all admire.
They can all our hopes inspire.
They can make our dreams come true.
Welcome the gang that can hack and hew.

Welcome the gang that can covet and snare.
They can make us free and fair.
They can stoke our greed and lust.
Welcome the gang that grinds to dust.

Gallows Song

For Father Delp, S.J.

We went north.
We went south.
We put our foot
Into our mouth.

We went in.
We went out.
We did not flinch.
We did not doubt.

We called it square.
We called it rough.
We did not fear
To call their bluff.

We spoke the truth.
We did not lie.
They strung us up.
They hung us high.

Gymnopédie

After Eric Satie

Saffron downs and downy naps:
Where the bare foot lifts and taps;
Shifts in tandem, sifts in tone,
Slips along the random zone.
Here the lithe and supple shades
Blend in honey-melon glades.
Saps imbue, pips permute
Budding tulips; carmine root
Lifting high its tensile shaft
Firm of flex, sleight of haft.
The air about is cool and rare;
The air about is lean and spare.
Pliant tendrils yet will glide:
Pliant petals seclude, subside,
Exude in coifed, enfolded sod
The sweet and fragrant milky pod.

Five Golden Rings

Five golden rings, the minstrel sings:
A golden wreath on golden wings.

At ocean's rim ascends and dips
A festive fleet of golden ships.

On distant hills the sun wakes up,
Pours dawn out of his golden cup.

Through shaggy crests the dolphins play
In cool sea-scuds and golden spray.

In noontide bayous may be found
A sad and lonesome golden hound.

The lamp burns low, the mosses droop.
A child whirls round her golden hoop.

The minstrel strokes his golden lyre:
Five golden rings, one golden fire.

The Frigate Bird

I can't fathom you, great frigate bird,
Black shard upon an azure sky,
Lancet of sunlit pales and plumes
Where pumice clouds rear coronets
And gilded pulpits crown the sea;
O ebon barb with fork-fletched tail,
Red-scarfed pirate, so they say,
Exerting your proud, imperious sway,
With pinions staved aslant the winds
You lord it over gulls and terns.
I don't know why, fleet "man o' war,"
You make me want to fly away,
To journey where white sunbeams fail
On your black moonbeams where you sail.

Scenes from the Rural Life

1.

Our Appaloosa mare has jumped her fence,
Stamps up and down on our back porch,
Bats the kitchen door with uplifted hoof.
She just wants to join us for breakfast.
Why won't anyone let her in?

2.

Do I have time to mourn even these:
A three-legged fox, half-starved,
Wobbling out of the woods nearby;
A crow, slapping black phlegmatic wings,
Peeling a squashed chipmunk off the road;
A recalcitrant skunk with a twenty-two slug
Deposited, regretfully, in its heart?

3.

Gimmicks of all kinds I bought
To keep the moles from tunneling my lawn.
None worked. Then a red-tailed hawk
Built a nest in my old oak tree.
I didn't know that hawks could dig.

4.

My guests enjoy the spectacle
Of wild turkeys strutting across my field,
Fluffing feathers, pecking hayseed as they go.
I enjoy it too; I'd enjoy even more
To have one trussed upon a platter,
Savory and crisp, stuffed with parsley,
Cornmeal, sage, and roasted chestnuts.

5.

I love my pear tree, its sweet, juicy pears.
So does a mother bear and her three cubs.
The cubs swing high through the branches,
Sending a rain of pears to their mom below.
It's prudent not to interrupt their feast.
They leave me a pear or two as consolation.

6.

I saw a bobcat pursue a rabbit.
I was glad to see the rabbit win.
Sorry, Willy Wordsworth!
Sometimes I think the "vernal wood"
Can't teach me much of anything—
Except to have a hole to hide me in.

7.

Fresh raspberries and peaches
In a sunny bowl;
Shall we still remember them
In December's wintry cold?

8.

The moose with thorny antlers
Glared at me with hostile eyes.
Then my stallion broke from a copse
And chased him into the woods.
I enjoyed being thought a horse
Guarded by the sovereign of the herd.

9.

The fox and the hawk had a standoff—
Both hankered for that dark-eyed mouse.
Both reckoned it wasn't worth the squabble.
The mouse scrambled off into my barn.
Now what am I supposed to do with it?

10.

I'm partial to dragonflies. My cat isn't.
She displays her web-winged trophies
In little iridescent rows along the patio,
After scooping them out of a summer breeze.

11.

On frozen nights when I went out
You reared up and tipped your snout
Switching the barn-lights on for me,
Kindly helping me to see.
Alas, alas, my porcine pal,
Remorse and shame hold me in thrall.
How many scoundrels in the end
Barbecue a faithful friend?

12.

I built an avian condominium—
A dozen little cubicles
With perches, doors, and sills.
I raised it high
Upon a stout and sturdy staff.
That was six years ago.
How did I err; how did I sin?
No grateful bird has ever deigned
To fly or nest therein.

13.

I was not surprised when I was told
How ancient Aztecs used to hold
That hummingbirds are recycled souls
Of fierce warriors slain and bold.
At my feeder I watch them fight,
Black arrowheads in lime-green flight:
They hover, swoop, dive and drub,
Deprived (thank God!) of axe and club.

14.

Red squirrels are tart and raucous chaps:
Unpleasant fellows, nature's raps.
They chatter, shriek, and scold all day;
They move inside our house to stay.
They never fail to make it clear
Who gets to give the orders here.
To all wood sprites I humbly pray:
Please make those red squirrels go away.

15.

I shooed, from time to time, one summer,
A yearling bear from my berry patch.
Shaking a mop, I would jump and shout.
He would leave, in his own good time,
Trundling casually up the hill,
Casting a scornful eye in my direction.
He seemed to say, "I'm departing to be civil,
Not willing to haggle with you just now.
If I were not, it would be you,
Mr. *Homo Sapiens* (so-called), and not I,
Who would depart, and not so casually either,
Running and hiding as best you could.
(And I have no mop to shake at you.)"

16.

Coy-wolves gather by my window
Yowling at the moonlit sky.
I kick the blankets off my bed
And arch my back in feral cry.

17.

I freshen the water in my birdbath,
And step inside to see what happens.
A fox slips warily from the woods,
Stands upright on his hind legs,
Perches front paws on the birdbath rim;
Then, like a *bon vivant* at his martini,
Slurps to his heart's content.

18.

I found that day a wounded doe,
Slumped against our fieldstone wall;
As from a scruffy duffle bag
Unzipped, eviscerated, torn,
Her entrails spilled upon the grass.
Her legs were pinned beneath her.
She pointed her tapered head at me:
Her black nostrils foamed with blood;
Her brown eyes were wide with fright.
I didn't know what I could do;
I crouched and knelt beside her.
She, who had ever shunned my kind,
Laid her head upon my lap and died.

Maritime Gallery

1.

Hidden shoals murmur from afar;
Mollusks, starfish, anemones, kelp
Undulate in clefts between the rocks.
Crabs explore the mossy ledges.
Porpoises scallop a distant bay
While frothy currents coil and curry
Spongy tresses in the hollows of the deep.

2.

That freighter from Brazil
Spilled a million roses
Into the foamy riptide
As it foundered there
Dashing its hull against a coral reef,
Discharging its bright cargo
Over dark waves and tumultuous seas.

3.

Coastal hummocks, mangrove, palm:
Pelicans glide over amber waves.
Coral outcrops here and there.
Two coconuts roll upward on the beach
Like dice cast from the fingers of the sea.
The ocean rim, like a sharp machete,
Splits a pink-guava sun in two.

4.

I won't contend with you,
Great-girthed, turbid clouds!
Spread your flocculent canopies
Over these tidal flats and pools,
These capes of fern and heather!
Allay these blatant skies, their bluster:
Festoon them with vertiginous convoys
Where mournful tears of men and angels
May daub the earth in vestigial dew!

5.

Lulled oceanic rotunda:
Fluted, ruffled, laminated,
Caressing softly at its fringe
Indolent thighs of flaxen shores.
Overhead, a topaz sky;
Cobalt-tinctured calms below.
A blur sways beneath the swells—
A snatch of flapping gulls engulfs it,
Plucking silver pendants from the sea.

6.

What more is there to say than this?
Ranks upon ranks of jagged ramparts:
Breaking, shuddering, thundering;
Sprouts of spray; shaggy spires
Assailed and crimped with spume.
Coastal jetties punched and harried.
Plumes of water spouting upward;
Startled sea-birds, glints of sun,

In frets and pools of massive boulders.
Offshore buoys pitch and bellow.
Who will heed their vain complaint?
What more is there to say than this?

7.

Grand croupier, smart in black cravat,
Aloof, encircling, glamorous sea,
With diamond studs and white-suede gloves
Deal out, draw in, as eddies flow,
Making currents ebb and tow,
Husks and shells, spines and spikes,
Old flotsam of our lives and loves:
Our wins and losses; losses, wins.
Shake out, suave sea, your green-felt scrolls,
While your game-wheel spins and rolls.

Faience

1.
Limoges

The tender palm of crimson dawn
Cups with clouds its silent yawn,
Dabs the napes of nimble limbs
With downy hues and sallow rims,
Embosses in bronze aureoles
Gnarled and antiquated boles.
Branches with fine tapered tips
Prime with rose the morning's lips.
Beams collide with sunny beams
And spar on cross-hatched pools and streams.
Here the marsh-grass dips and purls;
There bright convolvulus curls
In scarps and scarves so slight
It mimics arcs of wings in flight.
Semitones, aloof and spare,
Elude the brawny glint and glare,
Where cypresses, gaunt and dun,
Frame the vineyards of the sun.

2.

Chinoiserie

The autumn lodge brings cheer this day.
The plum tree blooms; the parrots play.
Cold rivers cleave far mountain walls;
Through narrow clefts, jade waterfalls
Plunge downward into misty lakes.
Geese and ganders, ducks and drakes
Like black strokes fleck the distant skies.
Over lowlands a heron flies.
A speckled horse drinks from a trough.
A woodsman totes his bundles off,
Traversing the vine-suspended bridge
That spans across from ridge to ridge.
Wine flags atop a bamboo pole
Flaunt a pavilion wry and droll
Wherein an agèd sage avows
Vermillion birds on golden boughs.

3.

Quimper

Mark this woman, mark this man:
Skirts and shirts in red and tan,
Ornate shawls, headdresses tall,
Togs and clogs both big and small,
Puffy sleeves and pantaloons,
Buttons round as pearly moons.
Note the lambs and prancing mares,
The ripe green apples, sorrel pears,
Blue roosters crowned with scarlet crests,
Golden hens in feathered vests;

Purple dewdrops, cows and things;
Sparrows swoop on stippled wings.
Gaudy ships on dimpled waves
Dot distant seas and gilded staves;
See some stout gigantic fish
Enthroned within his royal dish
Glazed with garish colors bright,
With parsley, cloves, and thyme bedight.
High upon the cliff-sides bare
Monuments and chapels rare
Bristle in the coastal air.
Mark Saint Mary, mark Saint Anne,
Mark the Christ of Paul Gauguin,
His yellow limbs, His arms outspread,
A thorn-wreath wound around His head.
Fiddle the porcelain viol and bow,
While children reap what angels sow.

4.

Meissen

The shepherd hides behind a tree,
Peeks out to see what he can see.
A pretty shepherdess, meanwhile,
Plumps down upon a silver stile,
Kicks off a slipper just for fun,
Laughs to see what she has done;
Reveals a rose-embroidered sock
Beneath her pert and lacy frock.
Overhead the chickadees
Chirp among the honeybees.
All gaze with happiness and glee
Upon this prim frivolity.
For nothing here shall be amiss
That can't be mended with a kiss.

5.

Haute moderne

Black eyes and beaks; banded rooks
Strut, fret, pout and pillage,
Pecking pea-pods, pitted soil:
Shingles, cockles, acorns, clods.
Chanterelles pock the grainy ground.
The sky is green, is tangerine.
Above the raw and rubble fens:
Earth is mustard, cobbled, gray.
Midway sprouts a chubby stem,
Clings aslant upon its neck
A global cerise-pleated bloom.
Chameleons clamped on craggy logs
Poke horny tongues into the gloom.
Grit, rags, dabs and bristle,
Rusty ferrules flit and prod.
Daws cant, caw and crackle;
Blackened claws; raucous grackles.
Tomorrow, yesterday, today;
All things awry; all things astray.

Willow Tree

Consolantem me quaesivi et non inveni.
Psalm 68

When I was by the dunes of grief,
   O Willow Tree,
I thirsted for your sap and balm.
But your roots had none to spare,
   O Willow Tree:
My lips were dry as bone.

When the noon-heat scalded me,
   O Willow Tree,
I pleaded for your cooling shade.
But your boughs were thin and sere,
   O Willow Tree:
No shadow but my own.

When my sinews ached with pain,
   O Willow Tree,
I sought your salve in dewy leaves.
But your twigs were harsh and bare,
   O Willow Tree:
Among briars I was sown.

When I raised my cry to you,
   O Willow Tree,
I longed to hear consoling songs.
But silence was all you had to share,
   O Willow Tree:
My song I sang alone.

Miniatures

1.

Monastic ruins:
A red bird swoops
Through vine-looped arcades.

2.

Footprints like blue roses:
Blue shadows on the snow.
Blue footprints like blue shadows.
Blue roses where I go.

3.

Plush plums, peaches, pears:
Children playing in the orchard.

4.

The tiger was the sunlight.
The peacock was the rain.

5.

Cinnamon and clover:
Twilight on the river.

6.

Down in the evening valley,
Village lanterns glow.
Fireflies sparkle
In the woods below.

7.

A jackal barks.
An ibis mounts the evening sky.

8.

The river is lulled.
It rains gently on the village.

9.

Gnarled and stunted tree trunks:
Guardians of the floodplains.

10.

Mallards paddle to an isle.
From tangled briars
They shall twill soft nests.

11.

Nightingales are silent.
Why do moonbeams
Hide behind the clouds?

12.

Who taught them how to do that,
Those ancient sages,
Casting silken nets around the stars?

13.

Three eldritch strangers came to sup.
We gave them each a precious cup.
They dipped their bread in blood-red wine
And lifted high their portions up.

14.

Can a poem about
A hummingbird
Be longer than
A single word?

15.

Pine bark, frayed, wet, decayed:
Rich banquet for a woodpecker.

16.

Drop, teardrop,
Upon a leaf in torrent's spray.
All the rains of India
Have come and gone today.

17.

Lions grow strong and tall
Like sheaves of wheat.
Guard well, O valiant leopards,
Your arboreal sanctuaries.

18.

Hinterlands blaze with hyacinths;
Lakes are green-gray slabs of slate.

19.

We stir with cramped
And crooked wand
A leaf-strewn, mossy,
Forest pond.

20.

Monarchs in sunny marquetry
Mull over lilac blooms,
Venting scents melodious
In lavender afternoons.

21.

Let the flutes be silent:
A bluebird sings
In the cherry tree.

22.

On that esplanade of sacral kings
I heard a donkey braying.

23.

Beneath a whitened shelf
Of starlit icicles,
A black wolf is sleeping.

24.

Pilgrims in a golden forest:
Old friends straying far apart.
Pathways, wending near and yonder,
Converge again amid the dark.

25.

Pine boughs limned
With scarves of snow:
Pennants agleam
In twilight's glow.

26.

Behold, those shaggy
Mountainous terrains
Where wild glacial ponies
Shrug their woolly manes.

27.

That mountain like a mother bear
Is humped in rage;
Foothills like her frightened cubs
Cower in her shade.

28.

I saw a heron
On the Nile;
The sun-bird floated
Half a mile,
Rose from her raft
Of woven reeds,
Bright Phoenix
From her home of weeds.

The Irish Brigade at Gettysburg

The cry of Ossar, Ossar the Hound.
Clash of youths, youths in slaughter.

"Fear not, my lads, the caissons' thunder,
Tromp of foemen in the haze;
Roadways parched, trees in flames,
Gaps and gullies, gorged with carnage.
Let staunch Hibernian battle-flags
Rise stoutly through fire-dragon skies!
Hear the clarions, bleating horns;
Cannons coughing loathsome spittle;
Gutted horses, shrieking, thrashing,
Entangled in their own entrails;
Muskets', side-arms' spurt and crackle.
Imbibe the stench of men and offal:
Arms, legs, bloody brains, and carcasses,
Heads like eggshells, popped and broken;
Ordnance scudding, flipping, jolting,
Mutilating the mutilated dead.
Fields littered, roiled, embittered
With splintered wheels, boots and sacks,
Love letters torn, cartridge casings, gore."

The cry of Ossar, Ossar the Hound.
Combat of warriors, warriors slain.

"Onward, lads, the battle luster!
Take back the orchard, grove, and vale!
Push back the foeman and his muster!
Make him think that Hell down under

48

Is a much less hellish place than this.
Love him as he loves you too,
Soul-mates in the love of glory.
May the valiant sons of Erin
Swing their emerald pennants high.
May shamrocks tucked in bonnets
Crown those who do not fear to die.
A bullet in the heads, lads,
Is but a headache fierce and fast;
Is then repose in gilded Cups
Where blood will blend with blood
Heart and soul, friend and foe
In the Heart of Hearts Himself.
Steeped forever in His keep."

The cry of Ossar, Ossar the Hound.
Fallen hosts, hosts of the dead.

The Fields of Asphodel

How could I detain you, austere shades,
In your roaming over sunlit pastures,
How impede your solemn promenades?
I have watched you browse and graze
Like extinct mammals of those ages past:
Woolly mammoths, aurochs, elks,
Wild horses prancing with high-plumed tails,
All tracing, in their far migrations,
Fault-lines of an earth already old.
Forgive me if I creep and scurry,
Dart in and out of groves and gulches,
Yelping like the savage of a savage age,
Denatured, disembodied, naked,
Battened on tattoos, bones, and beads,
Dulled by opiates and with flesh inflamed.
You are the bold, sagacious dead;
Your habitat, the realms of light;
I stalk you in my frantic haste,
Even as I shun you, flee away, and hide.
Grant wisdom, succor, to my flight.

The Mutiny

Call it mutiny, rude and vile betrayal,
A revolution of my bone and blood!
What grievances do you hold against me?
Did I not thank you, ligatures and joints,
When you bore me up among the hills
And mountains, source of joy and wonder?
And eyes, O eyes, eyes of my heart and soul
What gorgeous vistas did I deny you?
Why befog me now, leaving me half blind?
And ears that thrilled to robins, choirs, and fugues,
To laughter and to language and to truth:
Must you offend me, even as you bruise
My well-honed hearing with squeals and whistles,
Your own, self-made, grating sound?
Old faithful heart, why do you falter now,
Sagging, slogging pump, without just rhythm?
O limp my lungs and lax my loins and tendons!
I cough, I wheeze, my fingers crook and curl.
My palate mourns, bereft of nature's teeth!
And you, my brain, my precious brain,
Have I not nourished, fostered, pampered you,
Tried to make you learned, flexible, and strong?
Will you now conspire with that rebel crew,
Forsaking me, delivering me in bondage
To the rant of a vain, sputtering tongue?
O body, I have loved you all my life!
Even in the womb you were my loyal friend.
Your treason beckons me now to my end.

Reiter auf dem Ross

Ich sitze auf dem Leben
Wie die schlecte Reiter
Auf dem Ross.

Ludwig Wittgenstein

I sit, in pride, astride my life —
An inept rider on a horse.
The bridle-paths are dross and rife;
I ride, I chide, without remorse.

Yet I bemoan, disown this pace.
But not yet thrown, nor led astray,
I thank my horse whose equine grace
Alone, has shown, for me the way.

Marionettes in the Arbat, Moscau

Each piece to be accompanied by the appropriate music and dance.

1.

Pegasus

White wings, white mane, and long white tail,
Through crimson galaxies you sail.
Your neck is blue-veined travertine,
Your hooves of golden hyaline.
Your eyes like pale-blue planets gleam.
You race past Phoebus's vaunted team,
Churning up storms of diamond hail,
Asteroid cascades in your trail.
You gallop through webs the stars have spun,
Vaulting headlong beyond the sun!

2.

Gendarme

I know you're unwilling to confess
Virtues I may, or may not, possess.
You want me braver than I am,
Especially when you're in a jam.
You ask me to labor overtime
When you're the victim of a crime.
But when you opt to bend a rule

You'd rather have me play the fool.
You want me smarter, sharper, wise
When problems in your life arise.
But when you violate the laws
You find you rather like my flaws,
Wish me dumber, denser, blind,
No sleuth, no stealthy mastermind.
When along some wintry street
I tread my long and frozen beat
While in warm chair you backward tip
And through your murder novel flip,
Consider me and thank me too
That no arch felon dispatches you.
And when I lay me down to die
I know you will not sob or cry.
For though you will complain and chafe
My job it was to keep you safe.

3.

Petrushka

O what fears! O what bad dreams!
O how my life with dangers teems!
I scamper here and scurry there
All around the world's grim fair.
The Tartar chief, the Aztec priest,
The turbaned Moor, the big "blond beast"
Conspire to chase me up and down
To make me weep, poor motley clown.
Scottish war-pipes make me cringe.
Apaches can my brain unhinge.
An angry mob with noose and flare
Is just about my worst nightmare;
Mongol hordes' unleashed stampede;

The Foreign Legion's boldest deed;
Hungarian hussars' dolmens bright;
Cossack horsemen out at night;
Bengal Lancers in all their gear;
The towering Prussian grenadier;
Rome's tuba-braying legionaries;
Drum-pounding Turkish Janissaries;
British gunboats' cannons dire;
Mercenaries who kill for hire;
Samurai swordsmen's flashing blades;
Fierce commandos' daring raids;
Armed militias' "cleansing" bands;
"Holy" warriors' unholy hands;
Great armies roused by "righteous" ire
To slaughter, pillage, rape, and fire;
Viking ships and mounted knights;
Conquistadores and bombing flights;
Footmen armed with spear and pike;
The long-range missile's pinpoint strike;
The Macedonian phalanx;
Huge massed assaults of armored tanks;
Loud-shrieking mortars' plosive drop;
Deep-seeded minefields' bloody crop;
Greek hoplites in full panoplies;
Nuclear subs beneath the seas;
Fighter jets strafing refugees;
Guerillas, musketeers, dragoons,
Sappers, uhlans, airborne platoons;
Some hidden sniper's lethal aim;
Barns, villages, and homes aflame:
All of these and many more
Make my soul sick, my heart full sore.
I am so scared I hardly know
When to hide or where to go.
But, in the end, I can contend;

All perils in my life forfend.
I'll sway my hips and swag my head;
I'll scare away all that I dread.
The old folks said, "Fear not your foes:
Beneath the scythe the grass still grows."
Meanwhile, if this entertains,
Your applause will soothe my pains.
For now I droop and I must stop,
Into my puppet-box must drop.
I've met *my* demons tit-for-tat.
I bet *you* cannot boast of that.
(Please drop a penny in my hat!)

4.

Sorcerer

Take your staff, your arcane book,
Your peakèd cowl and gnarly crook
And conjure me a magic spell
That all my problems can dispel
And make my enemies run away
Or stoop in meekness to my sway.
I'll pay you with a handsome fee
As long as you serve up to me
My surly boss trussed like a swine
And pickled in a keg of brine.
And then my neighbor can be next—
Soundly hoodooed, soundly hexed.
That I think will do for now.
So sneer your lips and crimp your brow!

5.
Devil

Thump! Thump! Thump!
That's all it takes to make you jump!
Red-bedizened, leap and bump!
Snap your tail from bristly rump!
Shake your horns from hairy clump!
Stick your pitchfork in your hump!
Caper, cavil, carp, and slump!
We'll taunt you at the Final Trump!

6.
Chimney Sweep

Blackened hat, blackened cape;
Lanky shadow with blackened nape,
With sooty ladder, brush, and spade
You sidle by, a long, lean shade.
At too slow and grim a pace
With dusky mask and charred face
You stalk across our village square,
Burnt blemish on our thoroughfare.
Vanish down your ashy well!
Why don't you go right back to Hell!
When by the fire we're filled with cheer
Then we no longer need you here;
When our hearths are blazing bright
May demons roast you through the night!

7.

Prima Ballerina

Pizzicato, pirouette,
Petite curtsey, petite step,
Tap and titter on the stage,
Tilted arms and legs engage,
Eyes aglow, a vacant smile,
Elbows, knees, aslant awhile;
Spellbind us in a fairy trance
As we marvel how you dance.

8.

Persian Merchant

Gilt arquebuses, samovars
Daggers, jeweled scimitars,
Carpets ruby-red and blue,
Rugs of every shag and hue,
Brought from mountain, coast, and plain,
From every tribe and sheikh's domain;
A round and copper Turkish tray
With ewer etched and cloisonné;
Amulets against the Evil Eye;
Spices ground to gratify;
Limbecks, syrups, ointments fine,
Perfumes, pomades celandine;
Armenian goblets of brightest sheen;
Silken veils and shawls agleam.
Please sit down, inspect my ware;
Make your offer, make it fair.
Partake of *chai*, some *kaffe* too —
I can distill a potent brew —

Or (this we do not have to hide,
The Prophet will surely look aside)
A draught of arrack might well do.

9.
Snorkelbug

Don't you dare bamboozle me!
Don't you try to swindle my fee!
Eyes like goggles, ears like toggles,
Bandy-legged goblin who fumbles and hobbles.
Runt with a stunt! You grimace and grunt
With snarky nozzle so bulging and blunt!
Guzzle and slobber! Swagger and swill!
Shimmy and shuffle; rattle the till!
Prattle your cant, puff and pant!
Gargle your gullet with gurgling rant!
Swig your slop, shake out the mop!
Swivel the spindle, spin the top!
But don't you try to rankle my glee!
Don't you dare hornswoggle me!

10.
Two Skeletons

Don't fret the ghoulish escadrille
We dance upon this ghostly hill.
In life itself we had no stake;
Our flesh was for our pleasure's sake.
Now in fleshless bones we mate,
Our fleshless longings never sate.
Our bed is laid upon our biers,

Our boudoir is a tomb of tears.
We're lovers locked in endless hate,
Our spousal feast an empty plate.

11.
Fiddler

Fuzzy fiddler, make me cry!
Make me wring my hands and sigh!
Make me beat my breast to hear
Heart-throbs of my sorrows drear.
Draw that long and quavering bow
In melancholic adagio.
Tear my mournful soul to tatters
With trembling tones and muted matters.
Make me yammer, kvetch, and groan,
Blubber, snivel, sob, and moan.
And when you bow and doff your cap
I'll laugh aloud and loudly clap.

12.
Dervish

Orbit, pivot, eddy, whirl,
Make your skirts balloon and twirl!
Around the realms of spirit soar,
A flaring, human meteor;
Curl all created things galore
Into a cosmic pompadour.
Gird with splendor, gird with grace
The nameless Name, the faceless Face
Where at the onset angels flew
Harping the primordial Curlicue.

13.
Witch

Hence, wench, get out of sight!
Scram, you haggard, horrid blight!
Don't point your bony hand this way
Or shake your wand to my dismay!
With cat familiar and your broom
You'd better find another room
To bubble pots and make your brew,
Simmering a sordid stew.
Don't think your cackle cozens me!
Don't think I plan to come to tea!
I won't regret to see you soon
Swept off against the autumn moon.

14.
Archbishop

Like a little pleasure ship
With gilded sails that rise and dip
You navigate the vaulted nave
Holding aloft your crosier's stave.
All of us will hear with awe
The black-cassocked choir's caw
While like a mitered whitened dove
That nests in crannies high above
You gabble of Eternal Love.
You beck, you smile, you coo, you nod,
Exhorting us to worship God.

15.
Pugilist

You are young and you are tough.
You lend us youth and strength enough.
We've come to see you skip and jog
And beat the hell out of that slob.
Punch his paunch, hook to head,
Make him wish that he were dead.
Jab and clobber, twist and duck,
Smack the schnozzle of that schmuck!
Give the klutz a clop in kop!
Make him stumble; make him flop!
Avenge your neighbors and their brood:
It's payback time for every feud!
Help us triumph in our mirth.
Smash that nebbish into the earth!

16.
Matador

Upon the broad arena's sand
Against my bull I'll take my stand.
My cape will swish across his horns;
I'll baste with blood his tasseled thorns.
And when I make my final thrust
My bull will topple in the dust.
Brass trumpets will acclaim my pride,
My golden vest, sword tucked at side;
But pray for me that when I die
No bull awaits me in the sky.

17.

Pirate

A pirate fierce I was of yore,
Chugging rum and spouting lore
Of argosies and Spanish Main,
Of mariners drowned and seamen slain.
But now I spurn my pieces-of-eight.
I've scotched my eye-patch reprobate;
I've a better way to loot and sack
And be a good kleptomaniac.
I've traded in both cloak and boots
For Brooks Brothers three-piece suits;
Trim coiffure and blow-dried hair—
Fit headgear for a new corsair;
For shabby garb as buccaneer
I'll be a dapper financier.
For powder horn and blunderbuss,
For cutlass sharp and dangerous
I've substituted derivatives,
Junk bonds, hedge funds, and other sieves
To drain portfolios clear and dry.
O how my clients gasp and cry!
Davy Jones' Locker is my firm's name.
Who comes to me will sink in shame.
While I swim gurgling to the bank
Whole pension funds will walk the plank.
They give me leave to reinvest
Securities I think are best
(Though mainly in *my* interest).
Now should the market dive and crash
I've stashed as mine my clients' cash

(By sandy shores and ocean-reach
On "Treasure Island" in Palm Beach).
Skull and Bones will fly once more!
The Jolly Roger I shall restore!
I'll stab my poniard, stark and neat,
Right through the heart of old Wall Street.

18.

Dragon

I spume, puff, rage, and huff,
Snort and stamp and show my stuff,
Blaze fire-storms wherever I go,
Reducing to cinders what's below,
But please don't stoop to call me names.
I'll roll right over, burst into flames.
After all, I'm very shy,
Poor flummox floundering in the sky.
My fierce incendiary way
Is just my means to have my say.
Yet when I flame, you turn and flee.
Why won't anyone listen to me?

19.

Commissar

Don't fret when we shave off your hair.
We're only trying to be fair.
When every head is shorn the same
We'll all rejoice in freedom's name.
We'll mould you then as best we can
Into the New Generic Man.

What is unique and what is true
Will vanish in the common crew
(Except for us who are in charge:
Our privileges will just enlarge).
But if you disagree a lot
We won't demur to have you shot
(And better yet — to serve the good —
We'll liquidate your neighborhood).
We'll prize you uniformly dead:
Equal lead in every head.

20.

Giraffes

Giraffes, giraffes, what can I do
To make the whole world cherish you?
White, milk-chocolate, honey-dew,
Tall, freckled flagstaffs, bright and true,
Towering high in cloudless blue;
Huge amber eyes, wide ears imbue
Your nubby crowns with winsome hue.
Munching, crunching, you idly chew
Those tree-top branches you pursue.
When thirsty, you somehow construe,
With lanky peg-legs bent askew
To lap the veldt pool's lustrous brew,
Crooking an eye to keep in view
A noontide lion's dozing crew.
Giraffes, giraffes, your merit's due;
I marvel, wonder, love you too.

21.

M. Monkey, M. Mouse

Monsieur Monkey, Monsieur Mouse,
You keep a rather crazy house.
You think it's fun to run all day
Through corridors and laugh and play.
You tumble up and tumble down,
Each of you a crazy clown.
You scamper over stair and sill
With voices joyous, loud, and shrill.
How would I join you, heart and soul,
In your wild antics, dear and droll,
And race around just as I please
Setting my heart and soul at ease.
Monsieur Monkey, Monsieur Mouse,
Blessings on this, your crazy house.

22.

Unicorn

Out of a moon-shaft I was born,
A sheer-white, pearl-white unicorn
With tufted hooves and ivory mane
Bearing aloft my spiraled vane.
In leafy woods on far-off hills
Watered by springs and diamond rills,
I savor my deep-blossomed trove,
Aromas of my haunted grove,
Where phosphorescent elves alight
Upon my hornbeam starlit bright.
I elude those hunters' raucous rounds,

Their pawing steeds and panting hounds,
To muse beneath my old oak tree
In realms of peace forever free.

23.
Pharaoh

Beloved Kingdoms were my share;
Dual sovereignty I could declare:
Papyrus fronds and lotus blooms,
Steep pyramids and royal tombs,
The Sphinx's enigmatic stare,
Its eyes notched blind by desert's glare.
Queen Nefertiti's sacred breasts
Bestowed the solar-god's bequests
As I declaimed my cosmic hymn
Praising the sun-disc's fiery rim
Whence it extends its thousand arms
Conferring *ankh* with open palms,
As all creation nests awhile
Over Amarna by the Nile.
On temple walls parade in files
Blue hippos, jackals, crocodiles.
My reed chariot, like a bird,
Sweeps over floodplains swiftly spurred
By horses, ostrich-plumed and bright,
Begirt by cheetahs' rampant might.
Anubis weighs his scales for me;
My barge floats o'er the Wide Green Sea.
I shun the Mountains of the West,
The Wounded Death-Eye's dark behest.
I seek the Mountains of the East,

The womb of earth's abundant feast.
"*Di d'git ankh*" blessed glyphs decree:
"Eternal Life be granted thee."

24.

Golden Cockerel

Squawk, pluck, cluck and strut!
Click your eyelids, open, shut!
Cockerel made of gears and springs
Pulled here and there by copper strings,
You snap your beak, you whirr and peck,
You crook your fine metallic neck;
Your silver legs clack to and fro
Inlaid with gold intaglio.
Pulleys make you hop and bounce,
Flap tinny wings and feathers flounce.
What golden egg could make you grow?
What mechanism makes you crow?
A brassy turn-key I must screw
To hear your "cock-a-doodle-do."
A brassy turn-key I deploy
To fill your heart, and mine, with joy.

Après Teniers

Grab! Yelp and scuff! "Guard this trestle!
Punch that felon! Grapple! Wrestle!
Rile him! Roil him! Clobber! Cuff!
Choke him by his churlish ruff!"
Above them dangle sprigs of thyme,
Thin herring fillets stiff with brine;
Long blackened eels on iron rungs.
Smoked slabs of bacon, mutton, tongues
Slung from the larder's oaken rafter,
While Katrijn's coarse and brazen laughter
Displays her culinary charms!
She thrashes with her brawny arms
Big thievish Claes who swaggers, flails,
Swats downy leverets by their tails,
Snatches ham-hocks from the beam,
Upsets a jug of clotted cream,
Knocks over crusty sweetmeat pies,
And crocks of pickled oxen's eyes.
But dauntless Katrijn wins the fray,
Thrusts the oafish dolt away,
Shoves him sprawling across the floor
And kicks him out the scullery door.
Meanwhile, beneath the hearth-fire's hood,
Old Willem snoozes by the wood,

Ignores the strife, the steaming froth
Of cauldron hot with cabbage broth;
Dreams of leek and codfish soup,
Of garlic rampant in its loop,
Of purring treacle, wings on cheese,
And roasted pheasants roosting in the trees.

"La Cathédrale Engloutie"

With apologies to Debussy

Not as enchanted as the legends say,
You sink, O grand cathedral, into decay—
In wreckage of industrial debris,
Not in littoral splendors of the sea.
Dumps, oil tanks, railroad sidings, rusty cranes,
Abandoned factories scotched with shattered panes;
Canals clogged with toxic sludge, trees bent and frail;
Refuse-strewn fenlands—soggy, rank, and stale;
Transmission lines, muddy perpetual dusks
Of smokestacks smoldering among the husks
Of slag heaps, and highways leading nowhere;
Roads blocked and littered with discarded ware;
Boilers, axles, girders, struts and clamps,
Twisted scaffolds, wires, pot-holed exit ramps;
Steep derricks spouting dim sulfuric flares
That flicker ever through the thick night airs;
Once thriving neighborhoods, now dens of crime;
Parks and playgrounds smeared with soot and grime;
Schools boarded up, stores empty and forlorn;
Placards, graffiti, billboards stripped and torn.
Then do we presume too much to prophesy
That your spires again will mount the sky?
Your bejeweled windows and brassy heights
Will reflect once more those morning lights

As in old fables of a dawn-lit sea
Rising from the depths in bright solemnity;
Your budding sculpted boughs will yet unfold
Glad promises so new, and yet so old.

The Gate Called Beautiful

Acts 3:1–10; Isaiah 35:6

The Gate Called Beautiful: hardly!
Once kingly crowned in gold and silver;
Now tottering portal to the temple court;
A Roman sentry bored, asleep,
Propped up against his spear
(No Roman he: a ragged tribesman maybe,
Press-ganged from some hovel in the desert);
A mob outside, pushing, brawling;
Food stalls hawking hash and kippers;
Sheep, cattle, clouds of flies,
Curs nipping at hocks of surly camels;
Bleating, lowing, snarling, cursing;
Some frenzied plenipotentiary jerk
Flogging his donkey through the throng;
Cobblestones slick with slime and dung;
The ill and blind, the halt like me—
Lame since birth, legs limp as cankered logs—
All slumped together in roadside gutters,
Yammering for pennies, scraps of bread.
Then that yokel pair from Galilee,
Elbowing, angling through the crowd,
Babbling in their uncouth brogue,
Water-bags slung from beefy shoulders;
One young, one old, *piscatores*,

Ponchos rancid with carp and bream.
Why did I cry out to them: "Help me!"
They gaped at me, I gaped at them.
The elder invoked a Name in blessing
(Of some vagabond Nazarite, I was told).
His right hand grasped and yanked me up.
I kicked aside my swags and litter,
Leapt after them like a deer,
Like a deer with glorious legs
Through the Gate Called Beautiful.

Four Literary Palimpsests

1.

Ahab in Hell

The *Pequod*, they presumed to boast, was doomed.
What did they know of doom, those dockside molls?
Tankards of swart rum was all they hankered for.
They'd get their dole of brine before we'd done.
I got mine: acrid liquor to sate my soul,
Impelling fury in my flagitious veins.
Should I be grateful for what I've suffered?
My ceaseless vengeance on the world I'd wreak
For having wounded me and made me bent
And lame without due prize or recompense.
Justice demands the world itself should perish.
Only evil can triumph over evil.
I feel no remorse for those who foundered.
The compound races of mankind deserve
No less — to be deluged in the rancor
Of their quarrels, their violence, their hate.
So I betook myself and all my rabble
To the rapacious ocean streams and tides,
Entrusting lives and livelihood and fate
To that lolling ship, swaggering on the waves,
Drunk as a sailor in his tavern's broil
And brawl. What did we have to lose but life,

Life itself, pale and paltry palaver,
A quilted shroud of pious platitudes?
"Were I the wind, I'd blow no more on such
A wicked, miserable world." O wind,
Tainted with "cindered apples" of a tree,
Fill my sails; unleash the "clamped mortar"
Of my mind, its chocks and masts gagged and stale.
I set tattooed Queequeg and his compeers
To perch upon their teetering shafts,
Eyes fixed to that calamitous horizon —
The wide-cambered, sharp-taloned sea
Recumbent around us, cramped with dread.
Did I seek my quarry? Did it seek me?
We met where antipodal worlds collide.
The Leviathan had thought to master me
But gave to me exactly what I wanted:
No quarter, no reprieve, no trite remorse.
That white maelstrom of parlous condemnation,
Breaching "gentle joyousness" and repose,
Swigged me and mine down to the very lees.
Was that the final freedom that I sought?
After that, what bondage could imprison me?
Eternity with its shapely plenitudes
I shun; I seek formless infinity.
In process without end, without intent,
I shall emerge, the cynosure of chance.
Randomness and hazard shall plot my course:
Nameless, insubstantial, vacant, hollow.
"O lonely death on lonely life" for me.
I shall have my way; I shall have none other.
Where I am now, I've always longed to be.
My utmost joy shall be my joylessness:
"My topmost greatness ... in my topmost grief ...!"
"From hell's heart ... for hate's sake ..." I damn myself.
All creation I'd banish from my sight,
To dwell inside myself, myself my dearest blight.

2.
Hamlet in Wittenberg

My summons to the north, Horatio,
Bodes no greetings, no welcome home for me.
Doleful funeral and a marriage both
Shall celebrate with a sole chorale
Life in death and death in life, bound alike
In misbegotten spousal parity.
What tawdry carnival does that portend?
I'd skid the hackles of an angry sea
To some remote, some chill barbaric isle
Before I'd nestle there amid the spurs
Of brittle cliffs and thrashing ocean sprays.
But fortune leads me forth, crook-necked fortune
Garbed glibly in its harlequin disguise.
I'll sing and dance in contorted measures,
I'll grimace in their faces, pout and twist
At those whose baleful destiny I share.
Upon what wilted banquet shall I feed?
The bloated globe vents causes and effects,
All catastrophic in the end, all blear,
All deafened to our noble dreams and hopes.
And thus we grope, in moronic impotence,
Through pantomimes, sordid and grotesque.
Horatio, my mate, my foil, my friend,
Dare I bid you thither to that rank fen
Where ferrets' teeth and rapacious claws
Pick at bones bleached bare in rusty armaments?
Shall I urge you shed your scholar's cowl, your gown,
Your old arcades and cloistered lecture halls,
Your subtle schoolman's artful dialectic?
What mummer's mask shall you have to wear
Among those distant fripperies so grim?
What capers shall you cut, what adjurations
Shall you prattle, so nimble, prim, and quaint,

To flatter a gorged and florid shamelessness
That squats and squeezes on its costive throne?
Oh, quibble if you must, frame arguments
With countless *sic*'s and *non*'s and meet rejoinders;
Palliate your skies with angels ever sweet.
But the gods, my good Horatio, are cruel.
Blood, blood, and only blood, blood of my blood
They shall exact in lust before their stony altars.
They will have it. Their bloodstained altar cloths
Will double as my cerements, my pall.
I shall not gainsay their lurid nourishment.
Let them imbibe their wine, and I my gall.

3.
Munchausen in the Levant: Ghazals

From east to west I spurn no escapade — I speak the truth!
Whoever should doubt this fine masquerade — he speaks the truth!

Paragon of all the world, chevalier of fantasy,
I rise to greet my destined accolade.

Far in the fabled Orient, across the sandy dunes,
Princes tremble to see their glory fade.

Hosts of the eastern lands marshal their battalions bright —
Armed dromedaries muster in parade.

Alone with hound, and sorrel mare, and matchlock poised and lit,
I affront the thunderous cannonade.

Pashas and emirs, khalifs and beys, sultans, khans and shahs
I parry with thrusts of my rapier's blade.

Though many flashing scimitars assail me on all sides,
I pause to primp my chapeau's plumed cockade.

A city of turbaned towers I find, and jeweled gates.
We gallop through a porcelain arcade.

My lean greyhound, with ribs so keen, barks and growls and lunges,
Affrighting the Vizier's cavalcade.

The Janissaries' troops are sealing off the old bazaar.
Peeling a quince, I scorn the barricade.

My sorrel mare, in caracole, rears on her mighty flanks,
Bounds over the citadel's palisade.

Then, within, I happen to spy a pair of lustrous eyes
Gazing through the palace's colonnade.

On maraschino pools I guide my silvery felucca,
Intoning my paramour's serenade.

In moonlit mists a rosebud drifts down through the perfumed breeze
Dropped from the seraglio's balustrade.

Through carpeted halls I deftly glide, past the sentry's post;
And I abscond with that delicate maid.

I bring her to a castle fair by the steep Euphrates
With golden eaves and ivory inlaid.

An elixir of pure jasmine buds, succulent and rare,
I serve to her in goblets hewn from jade.

On eagle's back, from Pamir's peaks, I bring across the steppes
Snowy sherbets sheathed in silken brocade.

Now nabobs and sheikhs from far away, maharajas too,
Humbly solicit my valiant aid.

But all behests, though proffered by the world's great potentates,
Shall not outweigh our fountain's cool cascade.

From day to day, through seasons' sway, and years without number,
We'll sleep away in the tamarind's shade.

Under the stars and fruitful boughs, a lonely nightingale
Will celebrate our nightly promenade.

Munchausen indites this gallant tirade—I speak the truth!
Whoever should doubt this pompous charade—he speaks the truth!

4.

Quixote in Paradise

I rejoice among these scented hills,
Among these rivers of dark wine,
Among these fields of downy blooms
And heady spices, days unsullied
By the dross and drabble of age and time.
I, Alonso Quixano, erstwhile Don Quixote,
In La Mancha born and bred and buried,
Sifting my dust again into its soil,
Found gracious surety from my Liege-Lord
To journey hither to these blessed valleys.
It gives me leave to parse the filaments
Of my life, *of what was my life*; to bind
Its strands into one fine and plaited cord.
I was as I was warranted to be.
Who I was, even in my errant ways,
Magnified the seed that stirred my spirit
And the womb that gave me flesh of flesh,
Bone of bone, a proper investiture,
A place: in truth, a place upon the earth.
Shall I then grieve those dreams I entertained,
Dreams that bent my head awry, that led me
When it was I who should have been the leader?
I'll not reproach the vision that I had
Nor the course I traced amid its vagaries.
What more gorgeous vista could I traverse
Than when I, Rocinante, and Sancho Panza
Would tread the byways of serried Spain?
Stony outcrops crouched like tawny lions.
Skies were azure bays of glimmering light.
Rills were avalanches of chain mail
Glistering down through narrow mountain passes.
Aloes brandished thick and barbed blades.

Thunderheads, like wreathed bulls, scoured the plains.
Dawn would creep from bush to broom, day to day,
Stalking us, while the bleached and vaunting sun
Would thrust its golden targe across our paths
And the starlit snood of night would cull
Lush, earthly tresses in its purple snare.
We were all one glorious entourage:
Horse, helmet, burro, dangling sword and spear;
Proverbs, knightly lays, songs of love and longing;
Dulcinea, the beautiful, the proud;
Don Sancho, lordly viscount in the end
Of his demesne; Master Pedro's puppets,
Whose capricious antics I thought to tame.
But the swathe of my delirious sword
Cost me and others treasures bought too dear.
And I regret and shun the woeful day
When derisive chatelains paid homage
To my foibles, follies, confabulations
Grand, and not so grand. For I had fallen
Deep, and deeper yet, into boundless shame.
Were vanity, or madness, or contempt
My portion? How should I presume to know?
When trending homeward, raving in a cage,
Or taken sick unto my bed, I knew
The touch of mercy, the abode of grace:
By infirmity healed of infirmity
While my chivalrous deeds could yet attest,
Redounding in their very waywardness,
To what the faithful heart could strive to do.
How could I lament the gifts proffered me
Or the gifts I've given others in my way?

As the hyssop-sprigs of my repentance
I offer them to my sole Suzerain;
To Him alone, my valor and panache.
Who measures justly is Who measures me.
Beyond all fantasies, I've seen a star
Mark the heavens with its luminous trail.
This new world is more beautiful by far.
My quest begins again; I shall not fail.

Endnotes

Page 1: *Dumbarton Oaks* is the elegant Georgetown (D.C.) estate where, in late 1944, diplomatic meetings were held that led to the adoption of the United Nations Charter in 1945 and the promulgation of the Universal Declaration of Human Rights in 1948: two steps aimed at fulfilling Lincoln's dream of a polity that aspires to "do all which may achieve and cherish a just and a lasting peace among ourselves and with all nations."

Pages 3–9: *Aubade* (Dawn song); *Chansons des saisons* (Songs of the seasons); *Petite chanson d'amour avec bourdon* (Little love song with refrain); *Soliloque tragique* (Tragic soliloquy); *Fête champêtre* (Country festival); *Voyage fantastique* (Fantastic voyage).

Pages 10–16: *Kerch* is an ancient city on the Black Sea. The *Volga River* flows from north to south in central Russia. *Carmarthen* is a bay on the southwest coast of Wales. *Bordighera* is a small Italian village on the Riviera, quite close to the French border; the Metropolitan Museum of Art in New York City holds Monet's painting of the village.

Page 23: *Moritat* is the name given to a genre of traditional ballads that (often ironically) celebrate outlaws, bandits, or criminal gangs. "Mack the Knife" from *The Threepenny Opera* is the most famous modern example of this genre.

Page 24: *Gallows songs* are traditional ballads or poems as old, even, as the Middle Ages, wherein a presumed felon about to be hanged or just hanged utters his last words. *Father Delp* was a Jesuit priest falsely accused of participating in the plot to assassinate Hitler. He was executed a few days before the end of the Second World War.

Page 25: *Gymnopédies* are three piano pieces by French composer Eric Satie (1866–1925). The term means "bare foot" and refers to a dance in a classical Greek choral style.

Page 37: *Faience* is the name given to glazed decorated ceramic pottery. Limoges, Chinoiserie, Quimper, Meissen, and Haute moderne: this poem speaks of five standard forms of this pottery that have arisen from different national traditions, each with its own characteristic style and kind of subjects depicted.

Page 41: *Willow trees* are traditionally associated with sorrow and exile. *"Consolantem me quaesivi et non inveni."* (I sought consolation and could not find it.) This lament is from the Offertory for the feast of the Sacred Heart and Psalm 68 in the Vulgate.

Page 42: *Miniatures* here are grounded in Japan's Haiku tradition as well as in the forms of classical Chinese verse of the T'ang and Sung periods.

Page 48: *Ossar* is the mythical hound invoked three times in a battle hymn sung by the bard Ingcel in the Old Irish saga *The Destruction of Da Derga's Hostel*. The monument for the Irish Brigade at Gettysburg features a Celtic cross with a wolfhound at its base.

Page 50: *Asphodels* are flowers in the lily family that, in classical times, were said to grow in the Elysian fields and are thereby associated with the realm of the dead and mourning.

Page 52: *Reiter auf dem Ross* is German for "rider on a horse." The epigraph by Wittgenstein says, "I sit upon my life like a clumsy rider on a horse."

Page 53: *Arbat* is a colorful pedestrian street in Moscow known for its outdoor musicians, cafés, peddlers, entertainments of various kinds, and even puppet and marionette shows. *Snorkelbug* (an imaginary animal: a repulsive cross between a rodent and an insect); *Give the klutz a clop in kop* (Give that jerk a punch in the head!)

Page 69: *Teniers* refers to the seventeenth-century Flemish painter David Teniers the Younger, who is noted, among many other genres, for his rambunctious, comic scenes of peasants. This poem is based on a drawing in a private collection.

Page 71: *"La Cathédrale Engloutie"* is the title of a piano piece by Debussy based on the medieval legend of a cathedral once submerged in the sea that, one day, will resurface again in all its glory.

Page 75: *Palimpsests* are texts in a parchment or a manuscript that have been inscribed over another text. Each of the compositions of this collection makes extensive allusions to another text (*Moby Dick, Hamlet, Don Quixote*) or a tradition of tales (*Munchausen*).

Page 79: A *ghazal* is a traditional but extremely complex Persian verse form comprising a series of couplets, loosely connected. It may follow a variety of schemes. In this rendition, the first line of each couplet is fourteen syllables long; the second line of each couplet is ten syllables long and ends with a rhyme used throughout the poem. Both the first and second lines of the first and final couplets of the poem are fourteen syllables long and use the same rhyme as is used throughout the poem but internally on the tenth syllable and they end with the same final word. The first word of the first line of the last couplet of the poem, as is customary, announces the name of the speaker of the poem. Ghazals are quite difficult to write, but also great fun.

About the Author

Johann M. Moser was born in Cambridge, Massachusetts, in 1940. He grew up in New York City and later in New Jersey. At Dartmouth College he majored in philosophy and studied with the poet Richard Eberhart. In 1970, he received a Ph.D. in comparative literature from the Catholic University of America in Washington, D.C., where he specialized in poetics and medieval literature. From 1970 until his retirement in 2000, he taught literature and philosophy at St. Anselm College in Manchester, New Hampshire.

Moser published a volume of verse titled *Most Ancient of All Splendors* with Sophia Institute Press in 1989, as well as edited and translated for the press both an anthology of classical Nativity verse and, in collaboration with a colleague, Robert Anderson, an edition of St. Thomas Aquinas's hymns and prayers.

Although familiar with many areas of the United States and having lived several years abroad, Moser spent his early summers in the Lakes Region of central New Hampshire, where he has now resided for over half a century. In these decades, he has formed an intimate bond with northern New England, whose mountains and lakes and lively populace have been a source of inspiration for him, even as he has devoted himself to a sustained pursuit and emulation of world literature in all its dense historicity and its universal aesthetic achievements.

www.ingramcontent.com/pod-product-compliance
Lightning Source LLC
Chambersburg PA
CBHW031223120626
46545CB00003B/957